A comic and curious collection of animals, birds and other creatures

By BOBBIE CRAIG

MODERN PROMOTIONS
A Division of Unisystems, Inc.
New York, New York 10022
Printed in Canada

Aa *is for* ant, alligator, armadillo, ape and adder asleep in the afternoon.

counting animals

This is a highly entertaining collection of mammals, birds, reptiles and insects, past and present, seen in some very comic and curious circumstances. They are presented alphabetically and in glorious full colour. Children of all ages will have great fun identifying the animals in their strange situations.

Bb *is for* bear, badger, buffalo, beaver, boa, bandicoot, baboon and bison at a birthday party.

Cc *is for* cat, camel, cow, crow, cobra and crocodile counting cards.

Dd *is for* dormouse, duck, dog, deer and donkey dancing daintily.

Ee *is for* elk, eland, elephant, emu and eagle enjoying Easter eggs.

Gg *is for* gorilla, goat, gerbil, giraffe and gull gathering grapes.

Hh *is for* hamsters, hippopotamus, horse, hedgehog, hyena and humming bird haymaking at harvest time.

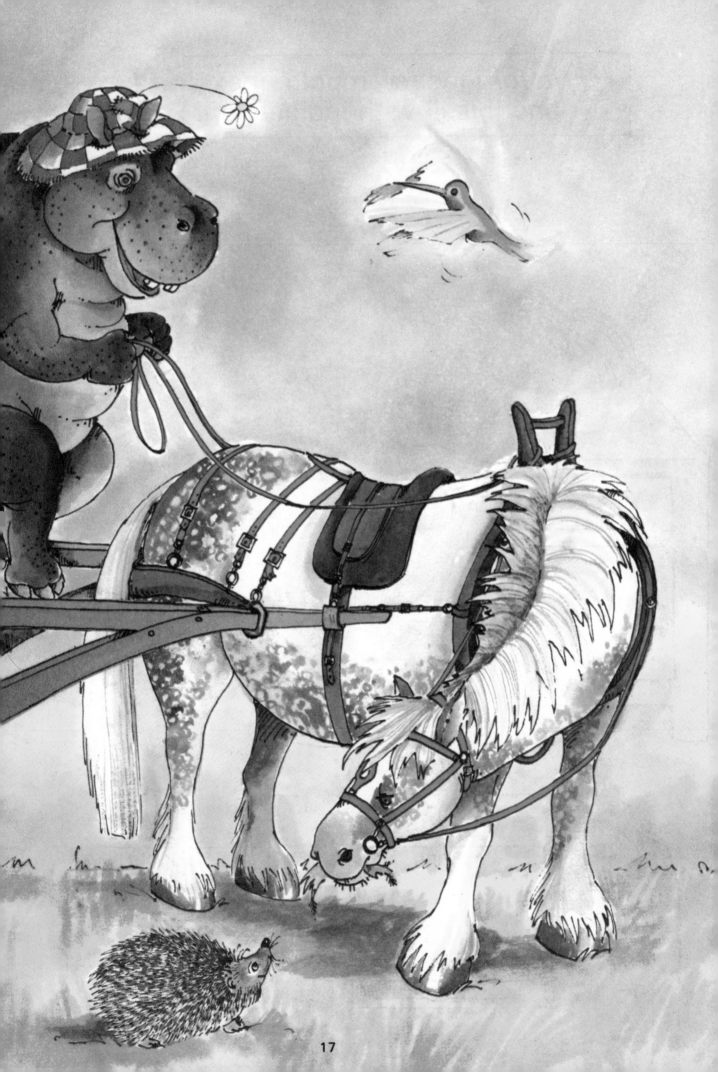

Ii *is for* iguana, impala, ibex and ibis ill with indigestion.

iguana

impala

ibex

ibis

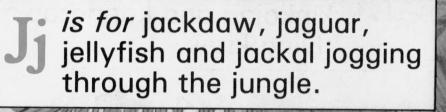

Jj *is for* jackdaw, jaguar, jellyfish and jackal jogging through the jungle.

Kk *is for* kestrel, kudu, koala, kinkajou and kangaroo flying kites.

L l *is for* lion, llama, ladybug, lynx, lapwing, lizard and leopard lounging by the lake.

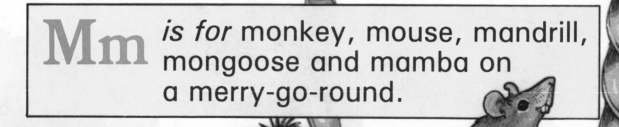

Mm *is for* monkey, mouse, mandrill, mongoose and mamba on a merry-go-round.

Dobbin

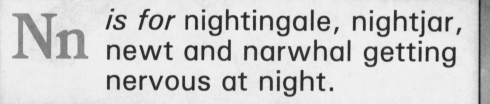

Nn *is for* nightingale, nightjar, newt and narwhal getting nervous at night.

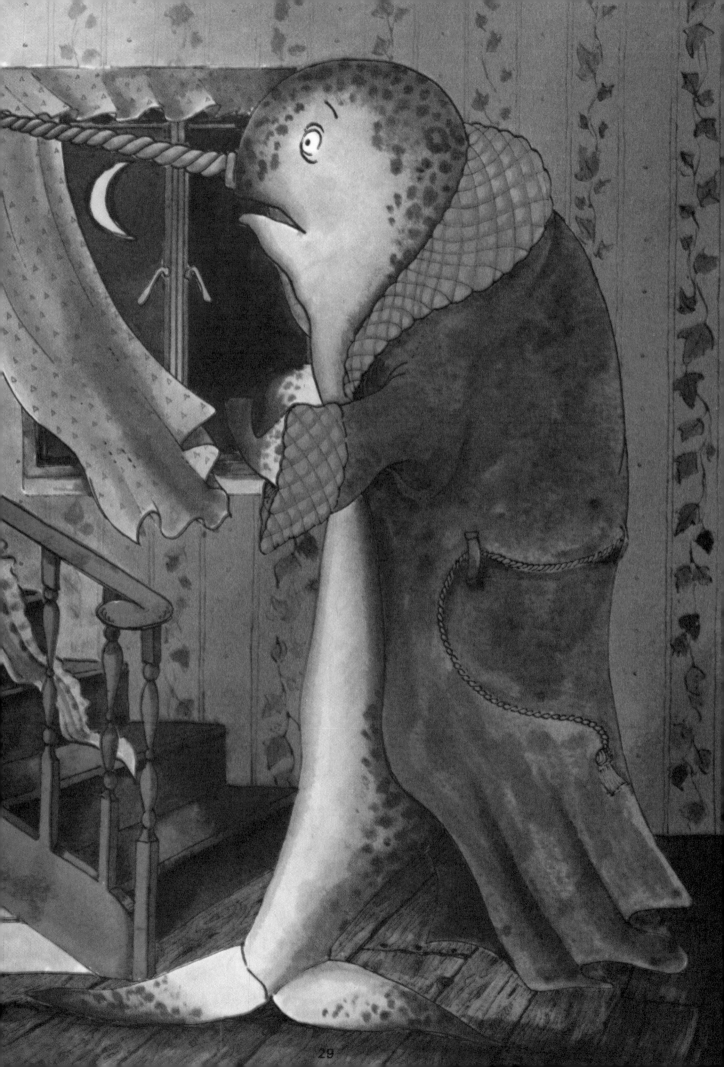

Oo

is for ox, opossum, otter, octopus, orang-utan, okapi and ostrich in an orchestra.

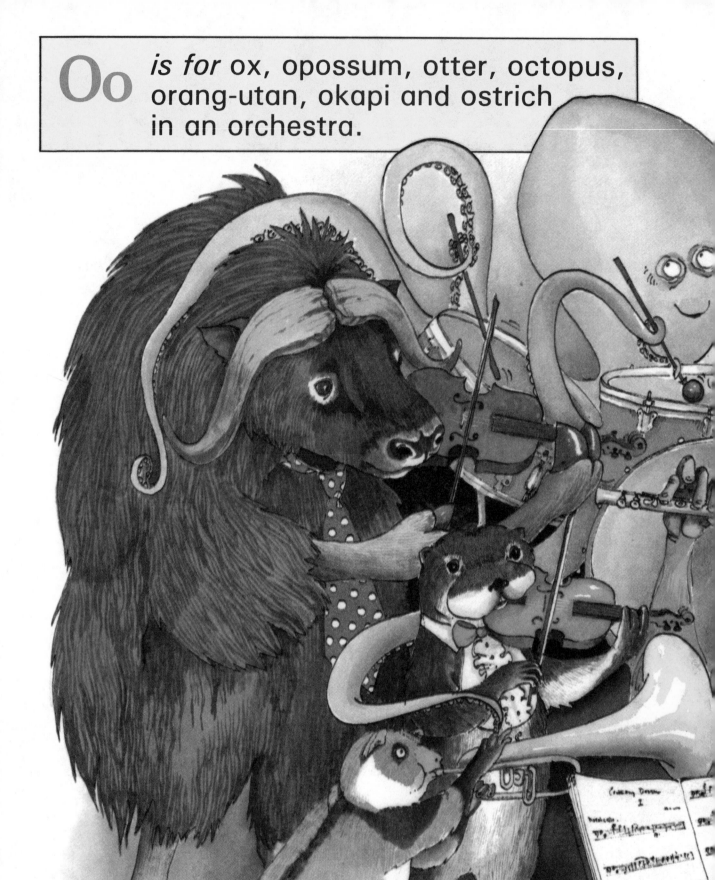

Pp *is for* puma, panda, pelican, penguin, pigeon and pig painting pictures.

Qq *is for* quagga, quails and quetzal queuing to see the queen bee.

Rr *is for* rat, rattlesnake, razorbill, rhinoceros and rabbit running in a race.

Ss *is for* squirrel, seal, snail, stoat, skunk and scorpion sunbathing on the seashore.

Tt *is for* turkey, toucan, toad, tweeter, turtle and trout tobogganing in twos.

Uu *is for* urchin, umbrella bird and uakari under umbrellas.

Vv *is for* vole, viper and vicuna looking at various vests.

SALE OF
VESTS
VARIOUS SIZES

W w *is for* wallaby, warthog, walrus, woodpecker, wolf, and weasels washing on a windy day.

Xx *as in* ox and fox examining x-rays.

46

Yy *is for* yaffingale, yak and yellowhammer yawning in their beds.

Zz *is for* zebras zigzagging at the zoo.

Tired tiger
telling us
that's the end

Laughing lion longing to learn to count

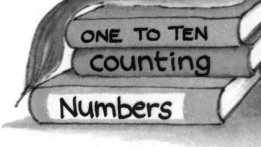

ONE TO TEN
counting

Numbers

1 hippopotamus humming

2 dinosaurs dancing

3 hyenas hurrying

4 bears boxing

5 dragons drinking

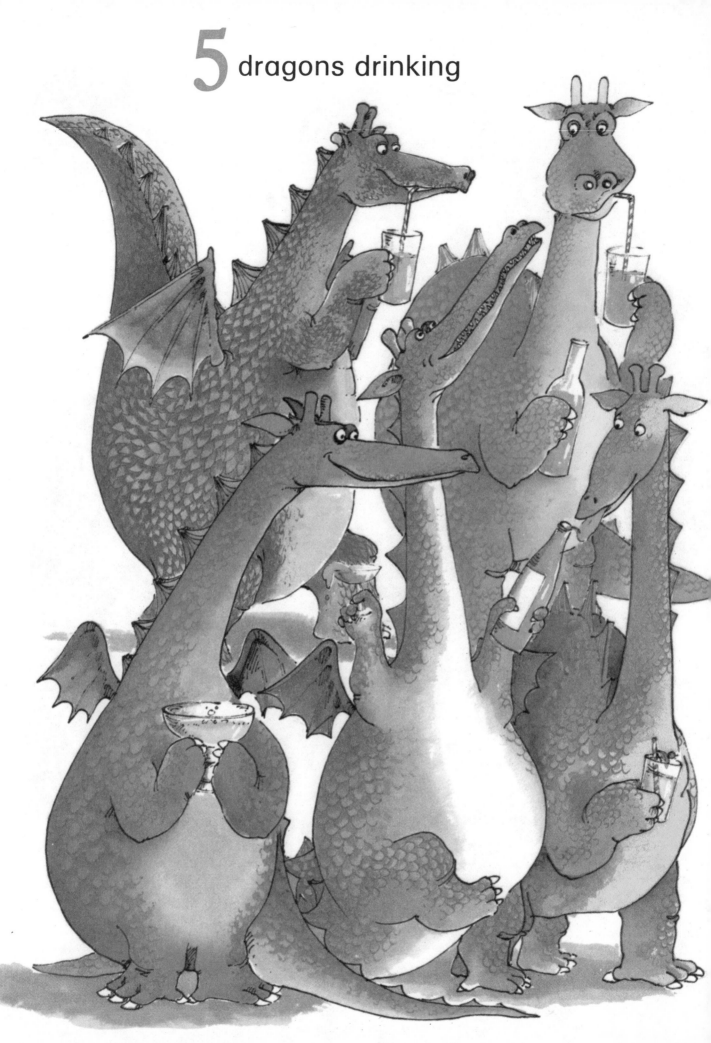

6 lizards leaping

7 snakes snoozing

8 penguins picnicking

9 monkeys making mischief

10 rabbits racing

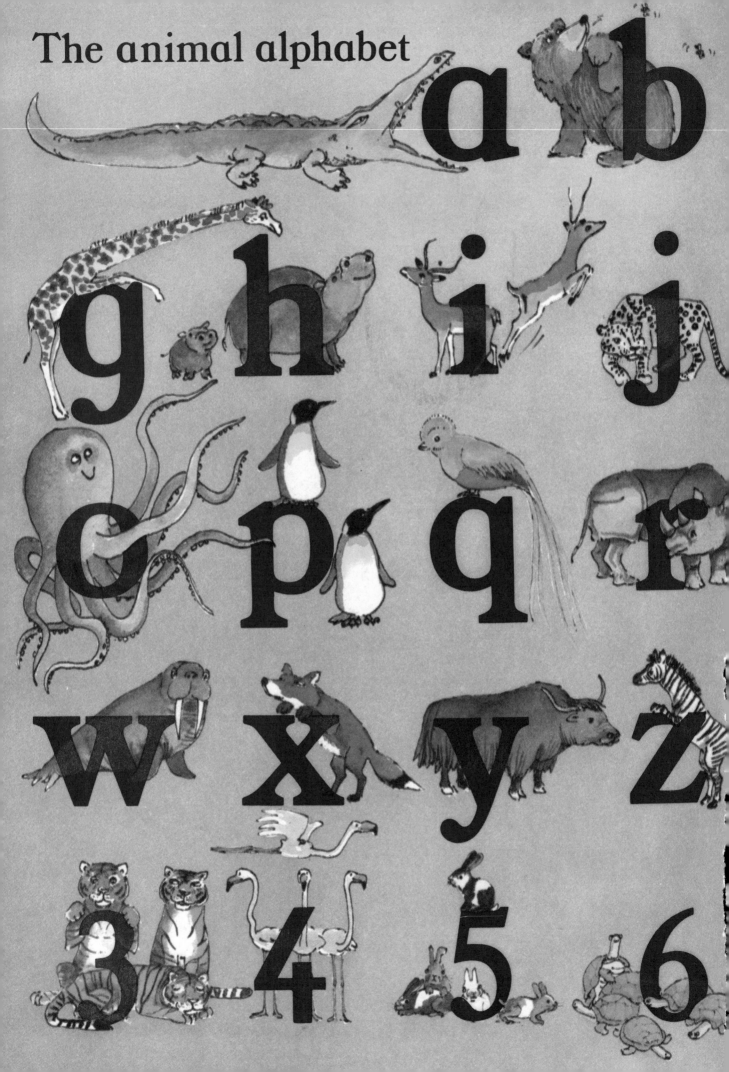

The animal alphabet